The Vesuvius Mosaic

LEVEL THREE   1000 HEADWORDS

UNIVERSITY PRESS

Great Clarendon Street, Oxford, OX2 6DP, United Kingdom

Oxford University Press is a department of the University of Oxford.
It furthers the University's objective of excellence in research, scholarship,
and education by publishing worldwide. Oxford is a registered trade
mark of Oxford University Press in the UK and in certain other countries

ISBN: 978 0 19 424829 7   Book
ISBN: 978 0 19 424787 0   Book and MultiROM Pack
MultiROM not available separately

Printed in China

This book is printed on paper from certified and well-managed sources

ACKNOWLEDGEMENTS

Illustrations and cover by: Levi Pinfold

*The publisher would like to thank the following for their kind permission to reproduce photographs and
other copyright material:* Alamy pp.7 (Roman tile mosaic/Holmes Garden Photos), 12 (Colosseum/
Alex Segre), 24 (Roman baths/Holmes Garden Photos), 33 (Roman tiles/Photolocate), 38 (Roman
fountain/Imagestate Media Partners Limited – Impact Photos), 56 (Volcano erupting/Yale
Center for British Art, Paul Mellon Collection, USA/The Bridgeman Art Library), 64 (Pompeii/
Robert Whitworth), 65 (Mount Vesuvius/Powered by Light/Alan Spencer), 74 (The
Pantheon/Marion Kaplan); The Bridgeman p.39 (*Mount Vesuvius in Eruption*, 1817 (w/c on
paper) by Turner, Joseph Mallord William (1775-1851); Getty pp.18 (/Roman ship/SSPL/
Science Museum), 71 (fresco/SuperStock).

DOMINOES

Series Editors: Bill Bowler and Sue Parminter

The Vesuvius Mosaic

By Joyce Hannam

Illustrated by

Levi Pinfold

Joyce Hannam has taught English in several European countries including Greece, Spain, Turkey and the Czech Republic. She now lives in York, in the north of England, and works for the University of York providing language support for all nationalities. She has written a number of other stories for students of English, including *Ariadne's Story*, *The Curse of the Mummy*, and the retelling of *The Teacher's Secret* and *Other Folk Tales* in the Dominoes series, and *The Death of Karen Silkwood* in the Oxford Bookworms Library.

OXFORD
UNIVERSITY PRESS

BEFORE READING

1 Mount Vesuvius erupted in 79 AD during the time of the Roman Empire. Tick the Roman things. Use a dictionary to help you.

a gladiator fights ☐   **e** public baths ☐

b mosaics ☐   **f** democracy ☐

c the Olympic Games ☐   **g** statues of Zeus ☐

d chariot races ☐   **h** slaves ☐

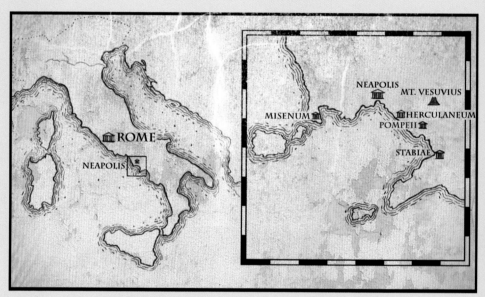

2 What do you know about the Roman Empire? Are the sentences true or false?

	True	False
a Many rich Romans owned slaves.	☐	☐
b The Roman Empire in 79 AD covered most of Europe.	☐	☐
c The philosophers Aristotle and Plato lived in Ancient Rome.	☐	☐
d Pompeii and Herculaneum were covered by ash after the eruption of Mount Vesuvius.	☐	☐
e The most important person in Ancient Rome was the king.	☐	☐
f The Ancient Romans thought that there was only one god – Jupiter.	☐	☐
g Ancient Romans invented paper and bicycles.	☐	☐

CHAPTER 1 ✎ A FREED MAN

'Hurry, Felix,' shouted Spurius. 'Let's finish this job and get home. Some visitors are coming from Pompeii tomorrow. Cassia says they may have some work for us.'

'It's nearly ready, **master**,' answered Felix, 'but I want to cut some **tiles** again. They don't fit as well as they should.'

'They look fine,' said Spurius.

Felix said nothing. He knew Spurius was careless. He didn't understand that every tile is important to the final **design** of a **mosaic**. But Spurius didn't design the mosaics. Felix did.

Soon they heard voices in the hall. Their customer was back home. Quickly Felix finished the last tiles.

'Where's my mosaic? Is it finished?'

'Come and see, Caius Calvinus Lepidus,' shouted Spurius.

Caius Calvinus Lepidus was an important man in Rome, a **senator**. He walked into the room to see the mosaic. Felix watched the customer's face carefully. Would he like it?

'It's more beautiful than I thought possible,' said Lepidus.

master you call the man that you work for this

tile a small, square things that people put on floors or walls

design this shows the colours and shapes in a picture before it is made; to choose the colours and shapes in a picture before you make it

mosaic a picture that is made from small tiles

senator an important man who decides what must happen in a country

1

Spurius laughed politely.

'I'm pleased, sir, that you're happy with our work. It's getting late, so we must leave now. My wife Cassia will send the bill later. We must **collect** Petrus, my worker, who's finishing a job nearby.'

'Won't you have some **wine** before you leave?' asked Lepidus.

'Another time,' answered Spurius, 'I promised to be home early, sir. You know how Roman wives can be!' He laughed weakly. 'Come, Felix.'

Felix looked at the mosaic for the last time. It was always like saying goodbye to a child you love. He put away his things and followed Spurius towards the hall.

Suddenly there was a strange noise and the floor seemed to move under his feet. There was a heavy, stone **statue** just beside Spurius. It started to fall towards him. Without thinking, Felix pushed his master away from the statue. It crashed to the floor near them and broke into pieces.

'Earthquake!' shouted Lepidus.

Then the noise stopped and all was quiet again. Spurius was sitting on the floor beside the broken statue. He was shaking.

collect to go and take someone or something from a place

wine a red or white alcoholic drink made from grapes

statue a picture of a person made of metal or stone

earthquake when the ground moves suddenly

'By the **gods**,' he whispered. 'It just missed me. Without your push, Felix...'

Felix found that he was shaking too.

'It's nothing, master,' he replied.

'This **slave** saved your life, Spurius,' cried Lepidus. 'Give him his **freedom**, man! I'll put my name to the papers.'

'Felix, I can never thank you enough,' said Spurius. 'From today you're a freed man.'

Felix gave his hand to Spurius. 'Can you stand, master?'

'Thank you, Felix, I'm fine.'

In the hall Lepidus's wife was counting their slaves worriedly.

Spurius and Felix didn't leave Lepidus's house for an hour. They needed to sit and talk about the earthquake. Although earthquakes were unusual in Rome, Lepidus explained that there had been more than usual lately south of the **city**. Nobody knew why.

It was evening when they walked to the house where Petrus was waiting. Spurius had Felix's papers in his hand.

god an important being who never dies and who decides what happens in the world

slave a person who must work for no money

freedom being free

city (*plural* **cities**) a big and important town

'What about that earthquake?' Petrus asked at once. 'I thought I was dying!'

'But you're fine. So is the job finished?' asked Spurius.

'Of course, master,' said Petrus. He was a freed man, a slave no longer, but he still called Spurius 'master'.

'He pays me, so it's safer to be polite,' he'd once told Felix.

'Show us the mosaic,' said Spurius. He knew Felix would notice any mistakes. Felix looked at Petrus's work.

'There's a blue tile in the wrong place in the sea and one of the green garden tiles is broken,' he said.

'Well, fix it quickly,' said Spurius. 'Really, Petrus, why can't you ever finish a job without mistakes?'

Felix didn't look at Petrus as he started work fixing things, but he could feel Petrus's eyes on his back, cold and hard.

On the way back to Rome, there was not much conversation in the **carriage.** Spurius was thinking about his narrow escape from death and Felix was looking at the papers in Spurius's hand. Was he really free? Petrus would be very angry about that, too.

When they arrived at Spurius's house, Cassia was waiting.

'Do you think this is a good time to return home?' Cassia asked.

'The earthquake made us late...' started Spurius.

Petrus and Felix quickly left the hall. They knew it was best to disappear quietly when Cassia was angry.

Spurius followed his wife to their bedroom. There he explained about the falling statue.

'Caius Lepidus made me give Felix his freedom,' he said. 'What could I do? He saved my life in front of the senator.'

Cassia's dark eyes grew narrower as she thought hard.

'We need Felix to stay in the business,' she said to Spurius finally. **carriage** an old kind of car that horses pull 'People know he designs the mosaics and they're starting to ask for his work. Now he'll stay with us for a time because he'll feel grateful to you for giving him his freedom. That's good! But how long will he stay if someone offers him a better job and more money?'

She stopped speaking and drank from the cup beside the bed.

'I have an idea,' she continued, 'Flavia must marry Felix. Then he'll be one of the family and we can keep his designs for ever.'

Spurius's mouth dropped open.

'Flavia, our daughter, marry a freed slave? Are you mad? She has very different ideas!'

Cassia laughed.

'Oh yes, she has other ideas all right! You don't see what's under your nose. She thinks she's in love with Petrus. If she's stupid enough to want to marry one freed slave, she can marry another. She must marry Felix for the business.'

Spurius was really too tired to argue any more.

'Let's sleep now, wife,' he said. 'We'll talk again in the morning.'

Cassia looked at his tired face.

'You sleep, husband,' she answered. 'I'll plan for the future.'

As Spurius fell asleep, Cassia smiled to herself. What a clever idea it was! The business would grow and her family would become rich and famous. The gods were helping her – even with their little earthquakes!

READING CHECK

1 Match the sentences with the people in Chapter 1.

Caius Lepidus ☐   Spurius ☐   Felix ☐

Petrus ☐   Cassia ☐   Flavia ☐

a He's Spurius's slave, and he designs and makes mosaics.

b He's a freed man who works for Spurius and makes mosaics.

c He's a Roman senator, the owner of the house where Felix has just finished a mosaic.

d She's Spurius's daughter and she's in love with one of his workers.

e He owns a mosaic business and Felix and Petrus work for him.

f She's Spurius's wife. She's often angry with her husband.

2 Are these sentences true or false? Tick the boxes.

	True	False
a The story starts in Rome in the home of a senator.	☐	☐
b Spurius and Felix are working together to finish a mosaic.	☐	☐
c Spurius and Felix are collecting Petrus when there's an earthquake.	☐	☐
d Spurius gives Felix his freedom after the young man saves his life.	☐	☐
e Cassia is angry that Spurius gave Felix his freedom.	☐	☐
f Cassia wants their daughter, Flavia, to marry Petrus.	☐	☐

WORD WORK

Complete the sentences with the words from the mosaic.

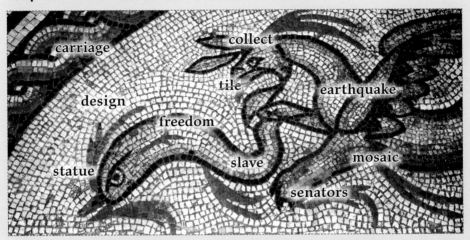

a There's a broken ......tile...... in the kitchen floor. Can you mend it?

b The .... of our new house is both modern and comfortable.

c This .... of a dog is made of more than one thousand small tiles.

d Roman .... were old men from rich families.

e There's a large .... of a famous writer in the town square.

f Many people died in the .... in Haiti in 2010.

g He worked as her ...., doing all the work without making any money.

h People should have the .... to choose where they live.

i I must go and .... my children from school now.

j The queen was riding in a gold .... pulled by six white horses.

GUESS WHAT

What happens in the next chapter? Tick three boxes.

a Petrus and Flavia ask Spurius if they can marry each other. ☐

b Spurius decides not to give Felix his freedom. ☐

c Cassia tells Flavia that she must marry Felix. ☐

d There's a large earthquake in Rome that kills many people. ☐

e Some visitors from Pompeii arrive to see Felix's mosaics. ☐

f Petrus thinks of a plan to make Cassia hate Felix. ☐

CHAPTER 2 ～ GRAFFITI

Flavia got up early the next morning. She and Petrus were planning to ask Spurius if they could marry each other.

But as Flavia was going to join Petrus in the garden, she met Cassia. 'Flavia,' her mother said. 'Come. I have something to tell you.'

Flavia followed Cassia into Spurius's office.

Minutes later, Petrus heard screams. Then Flavia ran out into the garden. Her face was red. Petrus took her in his arms.

'What's happened?' he asked.

When he heard about Cassia's plan, he was very surprised.

'You... marry Felix? But he's a slave and almost a child!'

'Mother says he isn't a slave any more,' cried Flavia. 'He's a freed man and she wants him to join the business as a **partner**.'

'What? A partner before *me*! And your husband!' Petrus cried.

'Calm down,' said Flavia, a little frightened. 'Everyone will hear.'

Just then, Felix crossed the hall on his way to see Spurius. He wanted to ask if he could go out and see Rome as a freed man.

'Good morning,' he said happily to Petrus and Flavia.

'Good morning,' replied Flavia quietly. Petrus said nothing.

'Oh dear! He's still angry with me about yesterday,' thought Felix as he went to find Spurius.

'What can we do about Felix?' asked Flavia when Felix had gone.

'Get rid of him,' said Petrus.

'But his mosaic designs are so good,' said Flavia. 'And mother thinks he's wonderful.'

'Then we must change her mind about him. What does your mother hate most?' asked Petrus.

'She worries all the time about what the neighbours think of us,' answered Flavia at once.

partner
someone who owns a business with other people

'That's it!' said Petrus. 'We'll write some really bad **graffiti** about her and make it seem like Felix wrote it. We'll say that she's

8

in love with one of the neighbours.'

'But Mother doesn't even like the neighbours!' said Flavia. 'Nobody will **believe** it.'

'People love hearing bad stories. And the neighbours don't like her much, do they? They won't mind if it's true or not. Cassia knows that.'

Flavia thought for a moment.

'It might work,' she said finally. 'Let's do it.'

'I'll write the graffiti this afternoon, when everyone is sleeping. Then let's see what happens to Felix!' said Petrus.

He **kissed** Flavia quickly on the top of her head.

At the same time, Felix finished talking to Spurius. He took his new papers and went out to enjoy his first day as a freed man.

Cassia was getting everything ready for their visitors from Pompeii. Some friends from Rome had told them about Spurius's mosaic business and they wanted to see some mosaics. They finally arrived an hour late.

Spurius, Cassia and Flavia were waiting for them in the hall, in their best clothes.

'Welcome, Bassus and Festus,' said Spurius as they came up the steps to the house. 'It's an **honour** to have you with us.'

Bassus, a tall man, **slapped** Spurius cheerfully on the back.

'Happy to be here at last!' he said. 'Come on Festus, my friend. Hurry up those steps!'

graffiti words in big letters that people write quickly on walls in the street for other people to read

believe to think that something is true

kiss to touch lovingly with your mouth

honour something that makes you feel special and pleased; to do something special to remember someone or something

slap to hit with your open hand

9

Festus couldn't walk very easily. Flavia wondered if he was ill.

'Would you like something to eat?' asked Cassia politely.

'By Jupiter, that's a good idea,' said Bassus loudly. 'The bottle of wine we had in the carriage hasn't done Festus any good!'

Festus arrived in the hall.

'Nice house,' he said to Spurius, 'but too many steps to the door!' Then he noticed Flavia. 'And who's this lovely young lady?'

'Let me introduce my daughter, Flavia,' said Spurius.

'Hello, my dear!' said Festus. 'Now did somebody say something about food?'

Cassia **clapped** her hands and the slaves brought the food to the **dining room**.

The meal was a strange one. Festus and Bassus were clearly **drunk,** but they asked for more wine. They got louder and louder. Flavia and Cassia were not speaking to each other. Only Spurius tried to make polite conversation. Bassus explained that he had very a special reason for wanting a new mosaic.

'I've been **repairing** my house ever since the last big earthquake seventeen years ago. It's nearly finished, but I need something really very special to finish the garden room,' he said. 'Then I'll have a big party there.'

'Good idea!' said Festus. 'Don't forget to invite me!'

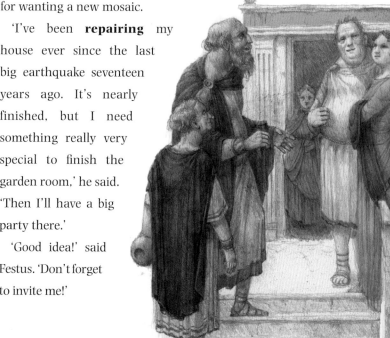

clap to hit your hands together

dining room the room in a house where people eat

drunk when someone has had too much strong drink

repair to make something that is broken good again

After lunch, the two visitors said they wanted to visit the nearly finished Colosseum.

'Do you want to see some mosaics before you go?' asked Cassia.

'No, dear lady,' answered Festus. 'After we come back.We want to see the Colosseum first. When the **gladiator** fights start there, we'll visit Rome often to see them.'

'Is the graffiti ready?' said Flavia to Petrus when the guests had left.

Petrus took her outside and showed it to her:

'It looks just like Felix's writing,' said Flavia. 'My mother's gone for a rest now. We'll see what happens when she wakes up.'

Two hours after that, the storm broke.

'Where's Felix?' screamed Cassia, red in the face.

'He's gone out, dearest,' answered Spurius. 'Why?'

Cassia took her husband to see the graffiti on the outside wall of their house.

CASSIA'S.
IN . LOVE.
WITH.TITVS.
GERMANICVS.
TWICE . AS.
OLD.AS.HER

'How could he?' she shouted. 'Me and that stupid eighty-year-old man next door? It's crazy! And to say I'm only half as old as him. It's too much!'

Spurius read the graffiti.

'I'll speak to Felix as soon as he gets back,' he said carefully.

'Speak to him?!' screamed Cassia. 'You'll do more than that! I never want to see his face again.'

gladiator a strong fighter that Roman people went to watch fighting other men or animals

READING CHECK

Tick the boxes to complete the sentences.

a The next morning Cassia tells Flavia …
1 ☐ that she can marry Petrus.
2 ☑ that she must marry Felix.
3 ☐ that she wants Petrus to be her husband's business partner.

b Felix thinks that Petrus is angry with him because …
1 ☐ he saw the mistake in Petrus's mosaic.
2 ☐ they both want to marry Flavia.
3 ☐ he doesn't like Felix's work.

c Petrus wants Spurius and Cassia to …
1 ☐ be angry with Flavia.
2 ☐ make him a freed man.
3 ☐ get rid of Felix.

d Cassia is waiting for some visitors from Pompeii who…
1 ☐ want to buy the nearly finished Colosseum.
2 ☐ want to see Felix's mosaics.
3 ☐ are escaping from the earthquake.

e When Festus and Bassus arrive, …
1 ☐ they are both drunk.
2 ☐ they want to see the mosaics at once.
3 ☐ they both fall in love with Flavia.

f After lunch, Petrus takes Flavia …
1 ☐ to watch a gladiator fight.
2 ☐ to see the graffiti he has written about Cassia.
3 ☐ to ask Spurius if they can marry each other.

g The graffiti about Cassia …
1 ☐ was written by Felix.
2 ☐ makes her angry with Petrus.
3 ☐ looks just like Felix's writing.

The Colosseum, Rome
Built: 72–80 AD

12

WORD WORK

Find words in the jars to complete the sentences.

a There's lots of ...*graffiti*... on the walls outside our school.

b He needs a new business .... because his old one just left.

c I don't .... in ghosts. Do you?

d She .... him on the face because she was angry with him.

e They drank lots of wine and by the end of the meal they were ....

f After the Colosseum opened, the Romans liked to watch .... fights there.

g The acting was very good and everyone in the theatre .... a lot.

h We had to .... the roof of the house after the storms.

t a f f i g r i

t r e n r a p

l e e b i v e

d l e p p a s

k n r u d

t r a i g l o a d

d l e p a c p

p r a i r e

GUESS WHAT

What happens in the next chapter? Circle the correct words.

a Bassus orders a statue / (mosaic) for his house from Spurius.

b When Felix sees the mosaic / graffiti , he wants to know who did it.

c Felix and Spurius / Petrus go to Pompeii with Bassus.

d On the ship, Petrus tries to push Spurius / Felix into the sea.

e Felix tells Petrus that he doesn't want / wants to marry Flavia.

CHAPTER 3 ∽ TO POMPEII

Bassus and Festus were both very happy when they returned from the Colosseum.

'There are no gladiator fights there yet, not until the building opens, so we've still got all our money,' they told Spurius. 'Show us your mosaics. We're ready to buy. Where's your lady wife?'

'She's resting,' answered Spurius. He hadn't seen Cassia since she'd gone to her room. He took the two visitors to the garden room and showed them Felix's mosaic on the floor there.

'That's beautiful,' said Festus. 'We have some wonderful mosaics in Pompeii, but I've never seen a better one than this. The design's clever and the colours are most unusual. Did you design it?'

Spurius was an honest man.

'My slave – no, freed man – Felix, did it,' he answered.

'Then I'd like to order one of his designs at once,' said Bassus.

Spurius looked very worried.

'Aren't you pleased with my order?' asked Bassus. 'I'll pay you well. What's the matter, by Jupiter?'

Spurius ordered some food for his visitors and asked them to sit down on a **couch.** Perhaps these men could help him with Cassia?

'I'm very happy with your order,' he explained. 'The problem is my wife. She wants me to get rid of Felix.'

'Is she crazy?' asked Festus. 'That young man's worth a lot of money to your business.'

Spurius showed them the graffiti in Felix's writing.

'Look, it's just a boy's **joke**,' laughed Bassus. 'That's what happens when you give a slave his freedom.' He thought for a moment. 'Listen. We'll take the boy to Pompeii to make a mosaic for me at once. Then your wife won't see his face for a while and she'll forget about this graffiti. We'll punish him with hard work.'

It seemed a good way out of the problem.

couch a long seat to lie on

joke something that you do to make people laugh

So that evening, Spurius told Felix he had to go with Bassus to Pompeii for a new job. He also showed Felix the graffiti.

'I never wrote that!' said Felix.

'But it's your writing!' said Spurius. 'You're lucky you still have a job. Just go to Pompeii and stay out of Cassia's way.'

Felix realized that Spurius didn't believe him. But who had written that graffiti and why? He had no idea.

Early the next morning, Felix was ready to leave with Bassus and Festus. As Bassus was getting into the carriage, he saw Petrus and Flavia laughing together.

'Does that man work for you, too?' he asked Spurius. 'I need this mosaic quickly and I could use another worker.'

Spurius looked at Cassia, who stood near him. She **nodded**. He realized she wanted Petrus far away from Flavia.

nod to move your head up and down

'Pack your things,' he said to Petrus. 'You must go with Felix to work in Pompeii until Bassus's mosaic is finished. I'll find other help here in Rome.'

Petrus stared. This was not part of his plan. Flavia turned white.

'Hurry up,' said Bassus. 'We have a ship to catch from Ostia.'

Felix wasn't happy either. He was hoping to get away from Petrus as well as Cassia. He had decided that staying in Pompeii for a while might be good for him. Petrus looked sadly at Flavia and went to fetch his things. What could he say?

'I'll write,' he whispered as he passed her and joined Felix.

At twelve, Bassus and his group caught a ship from Ostia to Herculaneum. Petrus was not speaking to Felix.

'I didn't ask Spurius to send Petrus to Pompeii,' thought Felix. 'So why is Petrus angry with me again?'

It was warm for the time of year, and as night fell, Felix went for a walk along the **deck**. It was a beautiful night and he felt happy to be away from Rome for the first time. His only worry was how to **prove** his **innocence** to Spurius. A gentle wind was blowing. It was wonderful to be free.

Suddenly he felt a strong man's arm around his neck. Someone was **attacking** him from behind and trying to push him over the side of the ship into the sea. Felix remembered something a friend had once told him. *If you're attacked from behind, drop to your **knees**. The attacker will fall with you.* He dropped suddenly to his knees and turned quickly round. He **grabbed** the other man's feet and pulled him down to the deck. Suddenly he could see the man's face in the moonlight. It was Petrus! His face was dark with **anger**.

'I'm going to kill you, Felix,' he screamed as the ship suddenly hit a big **wave** and moved over to one side. 'You can't have my job *and* my woman!'

'Your woman?' shouted Felix against the wind. 'Who's that?'

deck where you walk outside on a ship

prove to make people see that something is true

innocence when you have not done anything wrong

attack to start fighting

knee the middle of your leg; you move it when you sit or walk

grab to take someone or something quickly in your hands

anger you feel this when you are angry

wave a line of water that moves across the top of the sea

'Flavia, of course!' cried Petrus.

'I don't love Flavia,' shouted Felix. 'She's too old for me. And she's a Roman **citizen**! You're crazy!'

Slowly Petrus sat back on the deck

'But Cassia told Flavia to marry you,' he said. 'And Cassia wants you to be a partner in the business.'

Felix smiled.

'Me? A partner? That's not very probable. Cassia's sent me away to Pompeii because she thinks I wrote some crazy graffiti about her love life. Really, Petrus, I know nothing about her plans and ideas. And I'll never marry a woman I don't love, no matter what Cassia – or anybody – wants!'

Petrus looked **confused**.

'I'm sorry,' he said. 'I miss Flavia so much... I don't know what I'm doing. Good night, Felix,' he said, and walked slowly away.

Felix watched Petrus as he left. He felt **exhausted** after the fight. Petrus was a strong man.

'I need to think about this,' he thought. 'How can the two of us work together? I'll talk to him in the morning.'

citizen someone who lives freely in a country or city

confused not thinking clearly

exhausted very tired

READING CHECK

Correct the mistakes in the sentences.

a Bassus wants to ~~steal~~ *order* one of Felix's designs at once.

b Spurius is pleased because Cassia wants to send Felix away from the house.

c Spurius shows Bassus and Festus Felix's statue.

d Bassus wants Felix to go with him to Pompeii to repair a mosaic.

e Spurius shows Felix the letter and Felix says he didn't write it.

f Cassia is angry when Bassus wants to take Petrus to Pompeii too.

g Bassus and his group travel to Pompeii on foot.

h At night, Petrus attacks Felix and tries to kiss him.

i Felix tells Petrus that he loves Flavia.

j In the end, Petrus feels exhausted.

ACTIVITIES

WORD WORK

Correct the words in the sentences from Chapter 3.

a She walked into the living room and sat down on the **church**. .....couch.....

b We stood on the **desk** of the ship and watched the stars above us. ....

c He's very good at telling **smokes** and making people laugh ....

d I **robbed** my school bag and ran out to catch the bus. ....

e Nobody saw the thief, so it was hard to **move** who stole the money. ....

f It isn't safe to swim in the sea today. The **wives** are too big. ....

g When I fell over, I cut my right **key**. ....

h The army **packed** the enemy early in the morning. ....

i I **needed** my head to show that I accepted his invitation. ....

GUESS WHAT

What happens in the next chapter? Tick the boxes.

a When Bassus and his group arrive in Pompeii, they go …
1 ☐ to Bassus's house.
2 ☐ to see Mount Vesuvius.
3 ☐ to the baths.

b Petrus and Felix go into the city to …
1 ☐ drink some wine.
2 ☐ a tile shop.
3 ☐ meet a slave girl.

c In a street market, Felix sees …
1 ☐ a beautiful slave girl.
2 ☐ his brother.
3 ☐ an interesting mosaic.

d When Petrus and Felix arrive at Bassus's house, they …
1 ☐ have a bath.
2 ☐ have a fight.
3 ☐ meet Bassus's wife.

CHAPTER 4 ∾ SLAVE GIRL IN BLUE

In the morning, the weather was bad. Most people on the boat felt ill. Petrus stayed in bed until they arrived at the **port** of Herculaneum. There Bassus paid for two horses and he and Festus rode to the baths in Pompeii. Petrus and Felix walked at their side.

'Festus and I need a bath after that journey,' Bassus said. 'You two can come with us. I'll explain about the mosaic on the way. I want the design in two days and you'll have no free time until the mosaic is finished. You, Felix, may not leave my house because of your stupid joke in Rome. Petrus, you can go out only to collect tiles for the mosaic. I'll show you the shop you must use and I'll open an **account** there. But don't **waste** my money! Any questions?'

'Er...not at the moment,' answered Petrus.

'Good,' said Bassus.

They travelled to Pompeii in silence. There were big houses beside the sea, and the road – with **palm** trees beside it – was full of horses and their rich riders. Festus and Bassus were **chatting**.

'So much money!' whispered Felix to Petrus.

'Wait until you see the city itself,' Petrus whispered back.

The walls of the city appeared in front of them. They went in through a busy gate and passed some beautiful buildings before arriving at the baths. How rich these people of Pompeii were!

Inside the baths there were mosaics on every wall and floor. Felix noticed a beautiful, blue colour he had never seen before.

'Can we use that blue in our design?' he asked Petrus, as they held the **towels** for Bassus and Festus.

'It's a popular colour here in Pompeii,' replied Petrus.

'How do you know?' asked Felix.

'I've been here before, a long time ago,' said Petrus. 'I was a child then, but I remember the colour.'

Bassus shouted to them from the water.

port a town where ships can come in to land

account when you agree with a shop that they will write down everything you buy there and that you will pay at the end of the month

waste to use badly

palm a tree with wide leaves that you find in hot countries

chat to talk

towel you dry yourself with this after a bath

'Your mosaic must be ready by August 23rd. I'm having a party then and I've invited the most important people in the city. I want to be a senator and I'll need a lot of friends to help me do that.'

'Friends aren't easy to keep here,' added Festus.

Bassus and Festus came out of the water, and Petrus and Felix put the towels round them.

'Right,' said Bassus. 'Now listen carefully, you two. In my mosaic I want to see the young god of love, Cupid, and his mother Venus playing on the beach, with our mountain, Vesuvius, behind them. Felix, can you design that?'

'I can. Just give me two days,' answered Felix.

'Good,' said Bassus. 'Bring me the **drawing** when it's ready. Now let's go to the tile shop and open an account.'

'If you tell me the address, sir, and write a short letter to the owner, we'll go there for you and you can stay here,' said Petrus.

'You'll never find the shop,' said Bassus, surprised.

'I know the city a little,' answered Petrus. 'We'll find it.'

'Very well,' answered Bassus. 'Come straight to my house when you've finished. It's in the Street of Plenty. I'll take Festus home, and then warn my wife that you're coming. Don't lose Felix in the crowds. We don't want our designer to run away.'

drawing a picture made with a pencil or pen

Ten minutes later, Felix followed Petrus into the streets of Pompeii. The people spoke in a strange way, and some of them didn't look Roman. The shops were selling fruit and vegetables he'd never seen before.

'There are people from all over the **Empire** here,' said Petrus. 'Some come from the north, and some from Africa. You'll see lots of slaves from Greece, too.'

He stopped in a street market.

'I can't remember this square,' he said. 'It must be new.'

On the far side of the square, Felix saw a slave girl. She had a **basket** by her, and was buying some fruit. She had beautiful yellow hair and blue eyes. Her **tunic** was bright Pompeiian blue. Just then, she looked across the square and saw Felix. His heart jumped. She was so beautiful! The young woman gave him a small smile. Then she left the square with her basket of fruit. Felix wanted to follow her, but Petrus put a hand on his arm.

'I know where we are now,' he said. 'The tile shop's this way.'

The young woman disappeared. Felix had lost her. In a dream,

empire a number of countries that one country controls

basket a container that is usually made from thin pieces of wood

tunic a short piece of clothing that Romans wore which covered the body, but not the arms or legs

he followed Petrus to the tile shop and on to Bassus's house. Petrus talked about Pompeii, but Felix didn't hear a word. He woke up only when a slave opened the door of the house, and a tall, **proud** woman stood before him.

'Petrus and Felix, I suppose,' she said, looking at their dirty clothes and shoes. 'Come in.'

She turned to the slave at the door. He was tall and fair.

'Take these men to wash,' she said. 'Then give them something to eat and show them to an empty room near the slaves' room.'

She turned back to Petrus and Felix.

'My name's Rectina and I'm your **mistress** now,' she said.

As they followed the slave, Petrus and Felix saw Bassus in the dining room. He was drinking again, although it was still early in the day.

'Join me for some wine!' he shouted to Rectina.

'I have work to do,' she replied.

'She's as cold as a fish!' said Bassus, half to himself.

Petrus and Felix moved on. 'So,' thought Felix, 'Bassus and Rectina hate each other. It won't be easy living here!'

proud feeling special or important

mistress you call the woman that you work for this

READING CHECK

Are these sentences true or false? Tick the boxes.

		True	False
a	After their ship arrives, Bassus and his group travel to his house.	☐	☐
b	Felix can't leave Bassus's house alone because of the problem over the graffiti in Rome.	☐	☐
c	Bassus wants Felix to design the mosaic in two weeks.	☐	☐
d	Petrus was in Pompeii when he was a child.	☐	☐
e	Bassus wants his mosaic to show Venus and Jupiter with Vesuvius behind.	☐	☐
f	Petrus and Felix go to the tile shop to close an account there.	☐	☐
g	On the way there, Felix sees a beautiful slave girl with blue eyes.	☐	☐
h	Petrus and Felix go to Bassus's house and meet Rectina.	☐	☐
i	Felix thinks that Bassus and Rectina love each other.	☐	☐

WORD WORK

1 Circle ten more words from Chapter 4.

m	i	s	t	r	e	s	s	h
a	l	b	r	a	d	e	h	u
c	h	a	t	p	r	o	u	d
c	a	s	h	p	a	b	o	w
o	l	k	t	o	w	e	l	a
u	a	e	t	r	i	n	e	s
n	d	t	h	t	n	a	s	t
t	u	n	i	c	g	u	i	e
e	l	n	e	m	p	i	r	e

2 Match the words from Activity 1 with the definitions.

a ..mistress.. the woman that a slave works for

b .... you have this in a shop when you order things and pay later

c .... to use something badly

d .... to talk in a friendly way

e .... you dry yourself with this after getting wet

f .... a place where ships wait near land

g .... a picture made with a pencil

h .... a piece of clothing worn by the Romans

i .... a container that you can put shopping in

j .... feeling you are special or important

k .... a group of countries that are under one country

GUESS WHAT

What happens in the next chapter? Match the people with the sentences.

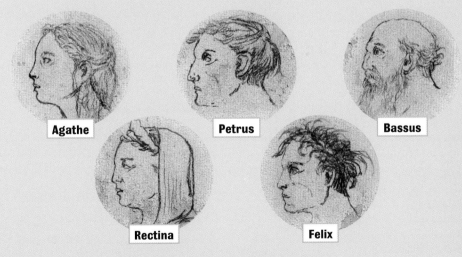

Agathe   Petrus   Bassus

Rectina   Felix

a .... writes a letter to Spurius about the graffiti.

b .... sleeps through a small earthquake.

c .... draws Agathe's face for his mosaic.

d .... comes back home drunk after the earthquake.

e .... works in Bassus's house as a slave.

CHAPTER 5 ∽ VENUS'S FACE

Later that evening, Felix and Petrus were chatting.

'What a wonderful city!' said Felix, 'But I'll never really have a chance to see it. How can I prove my innocence to Spurius and to Bassus? I never wrote that graffiti. But who hates me enough to write that kind of thing in my name?'

'You were taking everything I loved from me,' began Petrus.

Felix stared at him, surprised.

'So it was *you*! But why?'

'I'm sorry, Felix. I was **desperate**.'

'You must write to Spurius at once and tell him the **truth**!' said Felix angrily.

'I'll lose my job,' said Petrus.

'That's not my problem!' shouted Felix.

Just then, someone knocked on their door. It was the tall slave with some food for them.

'What's your name?' asked Felix.

'Alcander,' replied the young man. 'I'm Greek.'

'So, Alcander, could you please tell us more about the people we're working for?' continued Felix.

'What would you like to know?' asked Alcander.

'Well,' said Petrus, 'we already know that Bassus drinks. We saw that in Rome.' 'Yes,' said Alcander. 'The master drinks for two reasons. First, he was famous, handsome and good at sport when he was young. He used to drive a **chariot** in the **races** and he misses the life he had then. He often talks about it. Secondly, he married Rectina only for her money. She comes from an old, rich family and she fell in love with and married the young charioteer. But she soon realized he wasn't in love with her. He spent his time with other women. So she grew to hate him.'

'I see,' said Petrus, 'Thank you, Alcander.'

desperate
without hope

truth what is true

chariot an old kind of small, fast car that horses pull

race when horses run and the fastest horse wins

On the way to the bathroom, Felix saw a slave girl walking beside Rectina in the garden. She was wearing a bright blue tunic. As they turned the corner, the young woman looked up and saw Felix. It was the young shopper from the market! She looked as surprised as Felix was. Alcander passed by with some wine for Bassus.

'Who's that young woman?' Felix whispered.

'My sister, Agathe,' he answered.

For the next few weeks, Felix and Petrus worked hard. Petrus wrote and sent the letter about the graffiti to Spurius. They waited for an answer. Sometimes Petrus went into the city for tiles. He usually stayed out a long time. Alcander said that Petrus often met an older woman there, but Petrus never spoke of this to Felix. And Felix didn't mind, because it meant he had more chances to talk to Agathe alone. If Rectina was out, Agathe watched him while he worked. They chatted and laughed together. Alcander was pleased that his sister was happy and didn't **disturb** them.

disturb to stop someone from doing something

On August 20th, the weather was hot as usual. The mosaic was nearly finished, but Felix hadn't started Venus's face.

'You'll have to do her face soon,' said Petrus.

'The party's in three days,' added Alcander.

'I know,' said Felix, **blushing**, 'I'm just finishing the drawings.'

Agathe passed by with a cup of water. She smiled at them.

'Venus might have a sweet smile like that,' said Petrus. Felix laughed and blushed again. He couldn't hide his feelings.

Suddenly, there was a noise from under the ground, which started to shake.

'Lie down, everyone,' shouted Alcander. There was a scream. Agathe had dropped the water and **slipped** on the wet stone floor. She fell heavily to the ground.

The earthquake stopped after a few seconds, and all was quiet. Alcander jumped up and ran to his sister. Felix was just behind him. Alcander looked at Agathe's foot.

'Don't try to get up,' he told her. 'You've hurt your ankle. Felix, please fetch my medicines and some cold water.'

Alcander knew about plants which help people when they are

blush to become red in the face because you are shy or embarrassed

slip to fall when your feet suddenly move away from under you

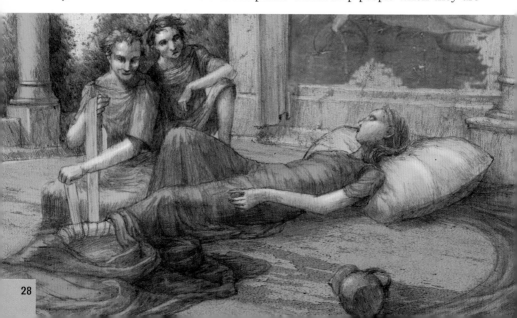

28

ill. His father had taught him many old Greek medicines. Felix ran to Alcander's room and came back almost immediately. But before Alcander could do much, Agathe began speaking in a strange, deep voice. Her eyes were closed.

'The god Neptune is angry,' she said. 'The gods will speak from the ground, the mountains and the sea. They'll punish us.'

Felix was worried.

'Wake up, Agathe,' he shouted.

'Don't,' said Alcander. 'She can't hear anyone. Just listen. It's dangerous to disturb her. This happens sometimes. She was born with a special **gift** from the gods. She can see the future.'

Agathe's eyes were still closed.

'Beware, people of Pompeii, you have wasted the gifts of the gods, and your life will disappear from the face of the Earth.'

'What does she mean?' whispered Petrus.

Suddenly Agathe's body shook. She opened her eyes.

'Alcander, what's happened? My ankle hurts!'

'There was an earthquake and you slipped,' said Alcander calmly. 'Now lie still while I **bandage** your ankle.'

'Thank you, brother,' she said, putting her head on the **cushion** that Felix had brought. Then she noticed the others.

'Why are you all staring?' she asked. She turned to Alcander. 'Have the gods been speaking through me again?'

'Yes... , but just rest,' answered her brother. 'Leave us now, please,' he said to Felix and Petrus.

Petrus went into the garden and Felix sadly followed him.

'What does she mean?' asked Petrus. 'I hate these earthquakes, but what Agathe said is terrible. The people here are rich, but they're not all bad. She can't mean they will all die!'

Just then, they heard voices in the hall. It was Bassus and Festus, and they sounded drunk again.

gift something that someone gives to you

bandage to tie a long, thin cloth around part of your body after you hurt it; a long thin cloth that you tie around a hurt part of your body

cushion this is soft and you sit on it or lie with your head on it

'Alcander,' shouted Bassus. 'Take my **cloak**! These young slaves are useless,' he said to Festus. 'One small earthquake and they forget everything. Just like all those **idiots** in the street, running around everywhere. Doesn't anyone remember what we had seventeen years ago? Now that really was an earthquake! These little **tremors** are nothing. Alcander, where are you?'

Alcander had finished putting the bandage on Agathe's ankle. So he went and took Bassus's cloak.

Rectina came from her room.

'Husband, what's all this noise? I was sleeping.'

'You've slept through a small earthquake,' replied Bassus.

Just then Rectina noticed Agathe on the floor.

'What's wrong with her?' she asked.

'She's hurt her ankle,' said Alcander, 'and can't walk.' He picked Agathe up and carried her to the slaves' bedrooms.

'Never mind her,' said Bassus. 'Is the mosaic damaged?'

Felix checked it.

'Just a little, sir,' he said. 'But I can repair it.'

'Then do it, and finish it,' said Bassus. 'A small earth tremor doesn't mean a holiday in my house!'

'Nothing does,' whispered Petrus to Felix. 'We need more blue tiles for the sea, sir,' he told Bassus. 'May I go to the shop now?'

'Not alone,' said Bassus. 'A letter came from Spurius this morning. He tells me you're the one who wrote that graffiti in Rome. Clearly I can't let you out alone any more. Felix is busy with the mosaic, so Alcander will go with you.'

Ten minutes later, Alcander and Petrus were on their way.

'Is Pompeii really in danger?' Petrus asked.

'What Agathe sees always happens,' answered Alcander. 'But we never know when. It could be years from now.'

'But what about the earthquake?'

cloak you wear this over your shoulders and around your arms and body

idiot a very stupid person

tremor a small earthquake

'Earthquakes often happen here,' said Alcander. 'It doesn't mean much. But there have been more than usual recently...'

When they reached the shop, it was closing.

'Earthquakes are bad for business,' said the owner. 'I'm going home like my customers. People are worried about their families.'

'Can we just take our tiles?' asked Petrus.

'Yes,' said the owner. 'But be quick!'

Once they were home, Alcander made a special drink for Agathe to lessen the pain in her ankle. Petrus took the tiles to Felix.

'Can you work without me for a while?' Felix asked. 'Festus has gone and Bassus is asleep. I want to see how Agathe is.'

When he arrived at her room, she was just finishing her drink. She smiled at Felix.

'Sleep now,' said Alcander. 'The drink will take the pain away.'

'Can I stay and watch her?' Felix asked. 'I need to make sure my drawing of her face is right,' he added. Alcander smiled.

'Would you like Felix to stay?' he asked Agathe.

'Yes, please,' she answered.

At the door to the room Alcander looked back. Felix was sitting with his pencil in his hand, quietly watching Agathe. Her eyes were closed and she looked very beautiful.

'Those two look right together,' Alcander thought as he left.

READING CHECK

Order the sentences to summarize Chapter 5.

a Felix and Agathe become friends. ☐

b Rectina wakes up and sees that Agathe is hurt. ☐

c Felix stays with Agathe and draws her face for his mosaic. ☐

d Agathe speaks in a strange voice about the future. ☐

e Petrus tells Felix that he wrote the graffiti about Cassia. ☐

f Bassus and Festus return drunk to the house. ☐

g Felix and Petrus meet Bassus's Greek slave, Alcander. ☐

h There's an earthquake and Agathe falls on the stone floor. ☐

i Felix learns that the beautiful slave girl is Alcander's sister. ☐

j Alcander and Petrus go to the tile shop to buy some blue tiles. ☐

WORD WORK

1 Complete the labels with new words from Chapter 5.

a s l i p

b _ _ a _ i o _

c _ _ u _ _

d _ a _ _ a _ e

e _ u _ _ i o _

f _ _ o a _

ACTIVITIES

2 Complete the sentences with the words in the tiles.

desperate   tremors   race   disturb   gift   truth   idiot

a I'm going to run in a .....race..... on
Saturday. I hope I win.

b It was late and I felt very tired. I was
.... to go to bed.

c You're not going to get on the table and
sing. Don't be an ....!

d Before the earthquake hit the city, they felt
some small ....

e Her wonderful singing voice is a real
.... from God.

f We have an important meeting. So please don't
.... us.

g I didn't do anything wrong. I promise you that I'm
telling the ....

GUESS WHAT

**What happens in the next chapter? Are these sentences
true or false? Tick the boxes.**

		True	False
a	Pompeii is destroyed by a big earthquake.	☐	☐
b	Felix tells Agathe that he loves her.	☐	☐
c	The Venus in Felix's mosaic has Rectina's face.	☐	☐
d	Felix plays a game with Bassus for Agathe's freedom.	☐	☐
e	Petrus discovers that Bassus is his father.	☐	☐
f	Petrus falls into a fountain and hits his head.	☐	☐

Chapter 6 ᔆ The party

On the day of the party, Felix started work early. He wanted to check that the mosaic was **perfect**. Bassus had put up a **curtain** in front. He planned to pull it back and surprise his **guests** in the middle of the party. Felix was not the only one up early. All the slaves were working hard, and Rectina was busy screaming at them.

By lunch time, it was very hot. Rectina went to her room to rest, taking Agathe with her. Felix finished his work and wanted Petrus to see the mosaic. But Petrus was not in the house.

'Someone brought him a message,' said Alcander, 'and he hurried out. We'll tell Bassus he's ill in bed if he asks.'

'Right. Well, would *you* like to see the mosaic?' asked Felix.

'Of course,' said Alcander. Together they went behind the curtain. Alcander studied the picture silently for a while.

'What do you think?' Felix asked worriedly.

'It's the most beautiful mosaic I've ever seen,' said Alcander. 'And the most beautiful Venus, too!' he smiled.

Two hours later, guests started arriving. They were all richly dressed. Alcander told Felix about them.

'That's a famous **general**,' he said, 'with his fat wife. The young man in the corner is a charioteer, the winner of this year's most important race. He's very famous in Pompeii at the moment. The old woman talking to him is the wife of a senator. He's not enjoying the conversation, is he?'

'He seems more interested in the girl over there,' said Felix.

'He's got no hope with her,' replied Alcander. 'Her father wants her to marry Rectina's uncle, Scissa. He's got the biggest house in Herculaneum. He's the man beside the **fountain**.'

'But he's **ancient**,' whispered Felix.

Just then, Bassus clapped his hands.

'Before we eat,' he said proudly, 'I'd like to show you all my new

perfect with nothing wrong

curtain people close these in front of something to stop people looking at it

guest somebody that you invite to your home or to a party

general a very important person in an army

fountain where water comes up strongly from the ground and falls down again

ancient very old

mosaic. Where's Felix? Pull the curtain, boy. Let's see your work.'

Felix shyly pulled back the curtain. His legs were shaking. Would all these important people like the mosaic? There was a short silence. Then everyone started speaking at once.

'Wonderful!' he heard. 'Really unusual work!' 'Look at the face of that Venus!' 'The blue of the sea is the best I've seen!'

Suddenly, a slave dropped a cup of wine. It was Agathe. She was staring at Venus's face. It was her own.

'Stupid child,' shouted Bassus. He lifted his hand to slap Agathe.

Suddenly, Felix came between them.

'Sir,' he shouted. 'If you like my mosaic, I ask you to play **dice** with me for the freedom of this girl. If I lose, you can have my freedom.'

The general spoke for the crowd of guests.

'It's a fair plan, Bassus,' he said. 'Let's all watch the game.'

Bassus couldn't refuse in front of his guests.

'Bring the dice,' he shouted.

'Three **rolls** of the dice,' said the general. 'The highest number wins.'

After two rolls, Bassus and Felix had the same number. Agathe was in the kitchen. She couldn't bear to watch. Bassus rolled for the third time. It was a five. Felix needed a six. Things didn't look very hopeful.

'How sad!' said the senator's wife. 'He's a brave boy.'

Bassus passed the dice to Felix.

'You'll be a useful slave,' he laughed.

Felix prayed to Jupiter, the king of the gods. Then he rolled.

'A six,' shouted the general. 'By all the gods, boy, you have some friends in high places!'

Alcander ran to tell Agathe. Bassus stared darkly at the dice.

'Time to eat,' said Rectina, quickly. 'Please choose a couch, everyone, and we'll have some food.'

At once, the guests started choosing their places to lie and eat. Nobody noticed that Bassus was still staring angrily at the dice and at Felix. Felix moved away and Rectina went to Bassus.

'It's only a slave girl,' she said. 'Go and talk to your guests. Don't you know how to lose a game yet?'

The slaves brought in **dish** after dish to eat. The guests started with **cheese** and eggs. Then there was chicken and many kinds

dice people play games of chance with these small six-sided things which have a different number on each side

roll when you move something by turning it over and over; to move something by turning it over and over

dish a plate of food

cheese yellow food that you make from milk

36

of vegetables. There were different wines with every dish and soon almost everyone was a little drunk. Some slaves started to play music and people began to dance.

Suddenly, Felix noticed Petrus coming into the garden.

'Where have you been?' he shouted to him over the noise of the music. 'We told Bassus you were ill.'

'I found her at last,' answered Petrus. 'But it's too late. She's dying.' He looked white and his face was wild.

'Found who?' asked Felix. He wondered if Petrus was drunk. 'I can't hear you well. Let's go to our room.'

'No. I must speak to Bassus,' said Petrus.

'Bassus is drunk,' said Felix. 'He's with Festus by the fountain. It's not a good time to talk to him about anything.'

'Let me go,' said Petrus, pushing Felix away. 'My mother said...'

'Your mother?' said Felix. 'She's here in Pompeii?'

Petrus walked straight to Bassus before Felix could stop him.

breathe to make air move in and out of your body through your nose and mouth

He whispered something into Bassus's ear. Bassus jumped back from Petrus and fell into the fountain. He hit his head on the statue in the middle of it on the way down, and lay in the water without moving. Festus stared at Petrus.

'What did you tell him?' he asked.

Petrus tried to pull Bassus out of the water, but he was too heavy to move. Alcander hurried to help, and together they pulled Bassus out. He was still **breathing**, but his eyes were closed.

READING CHECK
Match the two parts of the sentences to summarize Chapter 6.

a Felix finishes the mosaic …

b Alcander tells Felix …

c When Bassus shows his guests the mosaic, …

d Bassus is angry with Agathe and …

e Felix plays dice with Bassus …

f Petrus arrives at the party when …

g He looks wild and he says that …

h Bassus falls into the fountain after …

i Alcander helps Petrus …

1 wants to slap her.

2 Petrus whispers something to him.

3 people are starting to dance.

4 on the same day as the party.

5 Agathe drops a cup of wine.

6 to pull Bassus out of the water.

7 about the famous people at the party.

8 he must speak to Bassus.

9 to win Agathe's freedom.

WORD WORK
Circle the correct words.

a In England, people sometimes eat choose / (cheese) at the end of dinner.

b It was so hot that it was hard for people to break / breathe .

c Open those curtains / cupboards. Let's see the picture behind them.

d We can't play this game because we haven't got any dice / dance .

e There are no guesses / guests at the moment. The hotel's empty.

f The slave brought in a large chicken and rice wish / dish .

g There's a beautiful fountain / mountain in the middle of the town square.

h The gentle / general told all of the soldiers to stand in line.

i There are no mistakes in this report. It's perfect / perhaps !

j Can you roll / real the ball along the ground to me, please?

k My grandmother is really old. In fact, she's armchair / ancient .

GUESS WHAT

What happens in the next chapter? Tick three sentences.

a Bassus discovers that he's Petrus's father. ☐

b Felix and Agathe decide to get married. ☐

c Alcander doesn't want his sister to marry Felix. ☐

d Smoke starts to come out of the mountain near Pompeii. ☐

e Rectina decides that the family must stay in the house in Pompeii. ☐

f Felix and Alcander go to Rome for help. ☐

Vesuvius and the sea near Herculaneum

CHAPTER 7 ∾ FATHER AND SON

Few people noticed Bassus sitting on the ground. Most of the party guests were drunk and some had left. Petrus went over and sat down beside him.

'Open your eyes, Father,' he whispered.

Alcander stared at him.

'Your father...?'

'My mother told me he was my father,' said Petrus. 'She wanted me to know before she died. Rectina doesn't know anything about me. Bassus sent me away to Rome when I was a young boy to keep me a secret. And now he's dying,'

'I don't think so,' said Alcander. 'It's just the fall and the drink. He'll wake up soon.'

Morning was coming. A soft light was growing behind the mountain and the stars were disappearing. Rectina passed Petrus and Bassus on her way to bed.

'Drunk again,' she said, looking down at Bassus.

Felix and Agathe were sitting quietly together near the mosaic.

'You were crazy to play that dice game with Bassus,' said Agathe.

Felix smiled. He was tired, but happy.

'Now we can get married,' he answered. 'We're both free. Who can stop us?'

'I must ask Alcander,' she replied. 'He *is* my older brother.'

Alcander came up behind them with some water for Bassus.

'What do you want to ask me?'

'Can I marry Felix?' she said.

'Of course, and you can move to Rome with him,' answered Alcander, 'and have a new life there. But for now, you must sleep.'

As lunch time arrived, people started to wake up. It was very hot. The last guests went home one by one. Agathe woke up and ran to find Felix, who was sleeping in the garden.

'Wake up!' she shouted. 'Something bad's on its way.'

Suddenly, all the dogs started **howling**. Agathe fell into Felix's arms and her eyes closed.

'The gods are punishing us!' she sang in a strange, low voice.

There was a **huge** noise from under the ground. Everything started shaking.

'Look at the mountain,' whispered Agathe, opening her eyes.

Felix looked at Vesuvius behind them. Suddenly a **pillar** of white smoke came from the top of it. The noise continued. Bassus opened his eyes. and looked at Petrus.

'What's happening?' he asked.

'I don't know,' answered Petrus. 'I've never seen anything like it before, Father.'

Bassus stared at Petrus.

'Ah, yes. I remember now,' he said. 'You're Lavinia's boy. I sent you to Rome when you were only a child. Welcome home.'

howl to make a long, loud, high crying noise like a wolf or a dog

huge very big

pillar a tall thin thing that usually has a statue or the top of a building on it

Everyone, except Bassus and Petrus, was staring at the mountain. The earth stopped shaking, but the noise continued.

'Is it smoke?' asked Felix.

The white pillar went higher and higher into the blue sky.

'No,' said Alcander. 'It's **ash**. I've read about this in ancient books. Vesuvius must be a **volcano**.'

'What's that?' asked Agathe.

'A mountain with fire inside,' said Alcander. 'The fire in its heart comes from deep under the ground.'

As they watched, the smoke **spread** out over the sky. It looked like a big, white, palm tree.

Suddenly, they heard Rectina's voice. She was now standing close beside them.

'That ash is going to fall on us,' she said. 'My old friend **Admiral** Gaius Plinius has told me about volcanoes.'

It was the middle of the day, but the cloud above them was starting to cover the sun.

'We must leave at once,' she said. 'We must go to the sea and escape in a boat. The ash will cover everything. To save all the people, we need lots of boats. Gaius Plinius has many ships at Misenum. I'll write to him, and someone must take him the letter.'

'Not me,' said Bassus. 'I can't stand up and my head hurts.'

Rectina looked at him coldly.

'This is a job for strong, young men,' she said. 'Alcander can go because he knows the way to Misenum. And Felix must go with him. Get ready, you two. Take two of my horses – you'll travel faster

ash the grey stuff that you see after something has burnt

volcano a mountain that has hot fire in it which sometimes comes out of it suddenly

spread to move out from one place to other places

admiral a very important officer who tells sailors what to do

if you ride. We'll wait for you at the port of Herculaneum. Agathe, bring my writing things to my room.'

Agathe followed her out of the garden.

Small stones were starting to fall from the sky. One of them landed in the fountain.

'We must go inside,' said Alcander.

'Help me to carry my father,' said Petrus.

Together they took Bassus inside.

'I'm not going anywhere without Agathe,' said Felix.

'You'll have to ride under the falling stones,' said Petrus, 'It's not safe for her. And remember her bad foot. She can't ride a horse.'

'He's right,' said Alcander. 'We can't take her.'

He went out to find the horses.

'Felix, don't worry,' said Petrus. 'I'll take Agathe with Bassus and Rectina to the port at Herculaneum. You'll soon get there with the ships and we can all escape together.'

Felix shook his head.

'I don't like it,' he said.

Rectina came back with the letter.

'I found Festus sleeping in the dining room,' she said. 'So his carriage is still here. We can reach Herculaneum in that.'

Alcander came in.

'The horses are ready, Felix,' he said.

Agathe turned to Felix.

'I'm coming with you,' she cried.

'It's too dangerous,' answered Felix. 'You still can't walk well, and you won't be able to ride a horse. Petrus has promised to look after you. We'll meet again at Herculaneum.'

'Agathe,' said Alcander, 'please go with the others.'

'You're wasting time,' shouted Rectina. 'Look at the sky. There'll be no light soon. Go now – for the people of Pompeii!'

Alcander took Felix's arm.

'Come on,' he said. 'It's kinder to go quickly.'

The two young men hurried out of the room. Petrus held Agathe in his arms. She was trying to follow Felix and her brother.

Festus came into the hall.

'My carriage is ready,' he said. 'The streets are full of people and more stones are falling. We must leave at once.'

'Help me with Bassus,' said Petrus. The two men carried Bassus out to the carriage.

'Hurry,' said Rectina to Agathe. 'And stop crying. You'll have a reason to cry if a stone hits you. Can't you walk faster?'

They were now out in the street.

'Leave her alone,' Petrus said to Rectina. 'Or you can stay here by yourself. Your other slaves have run away already.'

'Don't speak to me like that!' screamed Rectina. Just then, a big stone landed beside her. She jumped into the carriage quickly. Petrus lifted Agathe gently into the carriage and climbed in after her. Festus hurriedly tried to start the horses, but it was difficult. The stones were hitting them and they were jumping wildly. Finally, they started to move through the crowded streets. People were running around alone or in groups. Many were looking for children or other people in their families. It was getting darker and darker, and the mountain was still very noisy. More and more ash was falling from the sky. When they got closer to the city walls, the streets were crowded with carriages. Everybody was trying to get out of the city towards the sea. After a long time they reached the Herculaneum **Gate** in the north-west, and when they arrived, they found people everywhere. Festus had to hit them with the horses' **whip** to get through the crowds. Children were screaming, men were shouting, women were crying, and dogs were howling. Some people were carrying bags of money with them.

gate a big door into – or out of – a town

whip a special long, thin stick that people use to hit animals

'Gods above, save us,' shouted Rectina, as they passed through the gate at last.

Festus drove as fast as he could through the crowds, but it was impossible to pass other carriages on the road. Bassus was lying with his head on Petrus's knees. His eyes were closed again.

Petrus looked back at Pompeii. He could see nothing except for the pillar of white ash coming out of the mountain, but he could hear lots of screams.

'It's like a picture of Hades, the land of the dead,' he whispered to Agathe. 'You were right. You saw this. The gods are killing the people of Pompeii. **Pray** for us now, Agathe. The gods may listen to you. It's our only hope.'

pray to talk to God

READING CHECK

1 Complete the sentences with the people's names.

> Agathe   Alcander   Bassus   Gaius Plinius   Festus   Felix   Petrus   Rectina

a .... tells Alcander the news about his mother and father.

b Felix asks .... to marry him now they are both free.

c Agathe wakes .... up to say she has a feeling something bad is going to happen.

d .... wakes up and realizes Petrus is his son.

e .... understands the volcano is dangerous and they must leave.

f Rectina writes to her friend, ..., who has many boats nearby.

g Rectina wants .... and Felix to take her letter.

h Bassus and the others travel in ....'s carriage.

2 Complete the sentences with names from the map.

a Bassus and Rectina's house is in ...Pompeii....

b A loud noise and a cloud of ash starts to come out of ....

c Rectina's friend, Admiral Gaius Plinius, has many ships in ....

d Petrus wants to take Bassus and the women to .... in Festus's carriage.

e Alcander and Felix have to ride to .... with an important letter.

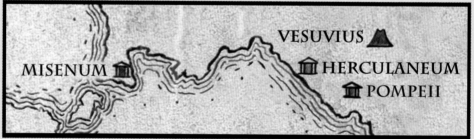

WORD WORK

1 Complete the labels with new words from Chapter 7.

a <u>ash</u>

b _ _ _ _ _ _

c _ _ _ _ _ _ _

d _ _ _ _ _ _ _

e _ _ _ _

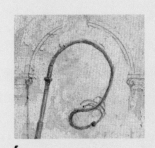

f _ _ _ _

2 Match the words and the definitions.

a howl   **1** to talk to God or the gods

b huge   **2** to move out from one place to other places

c pray   **3** a dog makes this long, loud, high noise

d spread   **4** very big

GUESS WHAT

What happens in the next chapter? Circle the words.

a Felix and Alcander find / don't find Gaius Plinius in Misenum.

b The ash from Vesuvius blows / doesn't blow south to Pompeii and Herculaneum.

c Plinius gets / doesn't get the Roman ships ready to sail.

d The ships reach / don't reach the port of Herculaneum.

e They save / don't save Bassus, Rectina and Agathe.

CHAPTER 8 ∽ THE ADMIRAL

Alcander and Felix rode fast through Herculaneum. It was darker and hotter because they were nearer to Vesuvius than before. The road was crowded with people going to the beaches.

'I know a quick way across the fields,' shouted Alcander to Felix. 'Come on! Follow me.'

They heard the sea before they could see it. Waves were crashing wildly on to the beach, and hot stones from the volcano were falling into the water.

'I've never seen waves like this,' Alcander said.

They both looked back towards the mountain. The pillar of ash was getting higher and higher, and the sun had disappeared.

'Let's go,' said Felix. 'We must find Gaius Plinius.'

They rode on to the north and into the wind. The horses were getting tired and they had to slow down. But, little by little, some light came back.

'Has it stopped?' asked Felix.

They stopped the horses and looked back. The pillar of ash was still there, and the fires on the mountain. But the noise was less because they were further away.

'No,' said Alcander. 'But look at the cloud of ash. The wind is blowing it south. It's covering Pompeii, but not here. We can even see the sun again.'

They rode back to join the road to Neapolis. It was still crowded with people coming away from Herculaneum. They were very tired and covered with ash. The people who lived in houses and farms along the road were watching the people on the road.

'What's happening in Herculaneum?' they asked.

'The end of the world,' answered one man. 'Stones and fire are falling out of the sky.'

'He's drunk,' said one farmer to another.

Alcander heard them.

'Leave your homes,' he said to the farmers. 'You're not safe here. If the wind changes, the cloud will come here, too. And the mountain hasn't stopped. The ash could easily cover all the country around here as well as the city itself.'

'You're crazy,' answered the farmer. 'Do you think we're going to leave our good land because a slave is afraid of a cloud?'

'It's no use,' said Felix. 'We're wasting time. Let's go on.'

A short time later, Felix's horse suddenly stopped.

'There's something wrong with my horse. I think she's stepped on something **sharp**,' he shouted to Alcander.

Alcander rode back to Felix and checked the horse's feet. In one of them he found a sharp stone. He pulled it out, but the horse's foot was bleeding badly.

sharp that can cut or make holes like a knife

'She can't even walk easily now,' said Alcander. He led the horse into a field beside the road.

'We'll both have to ride my horse,' he said.

Felix jumped up behind Alcander and they rode on again. Together they were heavy and the horse could only walk slowly. They passed Neapolis. Finally, they could see Misenum ahead of them beside the sea. But the horse dropped its head and stopped moving forwards.

'We'll have to walk the rest of the way.' said Felix.

At last, they reached Misenum. They asked for Gaius Plinius, admiral of the Roman **navy**, and they were sent to a big house by the sea. There were two **guards** outside the house. When they saw

navy a number of sailors who fight for their country

guard a man who stops people from going into a building

Felix and Alcander, they crossed their **swords** in front of the door.

Felix found his papers in the pocket of his tunic and showed them to the guards. Alcander gave them the letter from Rectina. As soon as he saw Rectina's **seal**, the big guard put down his sword.

'We come from Pompeii,' said Felix. 'This letter is for Gaius Plinius from his friend Rectina. The city is in danger, and our mistress asks for the help of the Roman navy.'

'Show them in,' said the big guard to the smaller one. 'Quickly.'

Felix and Alcander followed the guard into the house. The hall was huge and there seemed to be doors to lots of rooms.

'Where's the admiral?' the guard asked a slave.

'On the **balcony**,' answered the slave. 'He's watching Vesuvius.'

Felix and Alcander followed the guard to the balcony. An old man was standing there, looking out to sea. Across the beautiful bay, Vesuvius stood out clearly. The ash pillar was climbing higher and higher, and spreading fast south and east.

'Write this down, Pliny,' said the admiral to a young man at a table. 'The cloud is growing by the second and we can see more and more ash coming out of the top of the mountain.'

'Sir,' said the guard. 'Here are some men with a letter for you.'

'No time for letters,' said Gaius Plinius. 'This is much too interesting. We must write it all down for our grandchildren's grandchildren to read.' He didn't turn round.

'Sir,' said Felix. 'The letter is from Rectina in Pompeii. We've ridden as fast as we could to reach you. The people of Pompeii and Herculaneum are dying. They need your help.'

At last, Gaius Plinius turned and looked at them.

'By the gods,' he said. 'From Pompeii? You look half dead.'

Alcander replied calmly.

'In Pompeii it's like midnight. The cloud of ash has covered the sun. Stones are falling out of the sky and hurting people and

sword a long, sharp knife for fighting

seal something on a letter which someone must break to open the letter

balcony a place where you can sit or stand outside a building above the ground

animals. Everyone is running to the sea or hiding inside their houses. Please read our letter.'

Gaius Plinius took the letter from Alcander's hand and read it.

'Pliny,' he said to the young man at the table. 'No more writing today. Come and read this letter from Rectina.'

The young man went over to him with a pen in his hand.

'My nephew, Gaius Plinius Cecilius,' said the old man to Felix and Alcander. 'We call him "Pliny".'

'You've done well,' Plinius went on as Pliny was reading the letter. 'Now leave everything to me.'

'But... will you help them?' asked Felix desperately.

'Of course. There are thousands of Roman citizens in Pompeii and Herculaneum.' He looked at Alcander and smiled. 'And slaves too. I'll take my ships to Herculaneum as soon as they're ready.'

'Can we come?' asked Alcander. 'My sister...'

'I can't take any extra people,' said Plinius. 'Think how many

people I have to bring back.'

Then he looked at their tired, sad faces.

'Oh, all right, but I'll take the freed man only. It's the best I can do. I'm sure he'll find your sister.'

'I will, sir, I promise,' said Felix, and he looked at Alcander. 'You can be sure of that.'

'Good. Now go and eat,' said Plinius. 'We leave in half an hour.'

Felix and Alcander followed the slaves to the kitchen. Soon they were both eating.

At the same time Pliny was speaking to Gaius Plinius.

'Go Uncle, but be careful!' the young man said. 'Look at the sea. The waves are huge. We can't even see Herculaneum or Pompeii. How can you possibly find them and save the people there?'

'How can I possibly stay here?' replied Plinius. 'How can I tell the **Emperor** that the Roman navy did nothing while thousands of citizens died? I must try to save them.'

The admiral looked again at Vesuvius. Then he turned to Pliny.

'The cloud of ash is growing still,' he said. 'It's not safe here either. You must leave tomorrow morning at the latest. Take the road north to Rome and tell the Emperor what's happened. We're going to need his help when Vesuvius and the gods have finished with us.'

'Shouldn't I wait for you to come back?' argued Pliny.

'Listen, boy,' said Gaius Plinius quietly. 'We may not come back. I'm an old man. It doesn't matter for me. But you must write what you see, and remember everything for the future. Now get ready to go.'

Half an hour later, a slave found Felix still in the kitchen.

'The ships are leaving,' he said. 'The master says come now.'

Felix didn't call Alcander, who was sleeping.

'When my friend wakes up, tell him I'll find her,' Felix said to the slave. 'He'll understand.'

emperor the most important man in all the Roman lands

Soon after Felix arrived at the port, the ships left Misenum. They sailed quickly south with the wind behind them. Slaves pulled at the **oars** to help them move even faster. But as they came close to Herculaneum, it grew darker and the sea grew wilder and wilder. Huge stones fell into the water. The ships tried to turn into the port, but the sea was full of rocks and they were in danger. The sailors could hear people shouting, but they couldn't see the port. Falling ash started to cover the ships and the men. There was also a terrible smell like bad eggs.

'Back out to sea,' ordered Gaius Plinius. 'Run south with the wind. Save the ships. Sail for Stabiae.'

'No!' screamed Felix, who stood beside him on the deck.

'I'm sorry, my boy,' said the old man. 'There's nothing I can do for them. We must save ourselves.'

As the ships ran south with the wind, Felix and the admiral listened to the screams coming from the land. In his mind, Felix said goodbye to his beautiful Agathe. He would never see her again. Then, as they watched, a pillar of fire shot up into the air from the top of the mountain. It started to run down the side of the mountain towards Herculaneum faster than the wind itself. It looked like an angry **snake** and the smell of **gas** grew even stronger.

'Pull harder,' shouted Plinius to the slaves who were **rowing** the ships. 'This is no ordinary fire. It will burn everything in front of it.'

As he spoke, the snake of fire reached the sea. There was a huge noise and the water beside Herculaneum seemed to turn red and smoky. Luckily, the wind and the waves soon pushed them far away to the south.

'Gods above – they must all be dead,' whispered Plinius. And Felix realized that he could hear no more screams in the wind.

oar a long, wooden stick that you use to move a boat or ship forwards in the water

snake a long animal with no legs

gas something like air that gives light and heat when it burns

row to move a boat forwards with oars

READING CHECK

Tick the boxes to complete the sentences.

a As Alcander and Felix ride to … , they see the cloud of ash is blowing south.
1 ☐ Pompeii   3 ☐ Rome
2 ☑ Misenum

b On the road to Neapolis, they speak to some … who think they are crazy.
1 ☐ farmers   3 ☐ slaves
2 ☐ guards

c Felix's horse hurts its … and can't go any further.
1 ☐ neck   3 ☐ foot
2 ☐ tail

d When they reach Misenum, they are dirty and … .
1 ☐ exhausted   3 ☐ drunk
2 ☐ excited

e Gaius Plinius's guards don't want to let them into the … .
1 ☐ ship   3 ☐ house
2 ☐ hall

f After Gaius Plinius reads the letter, he decides to take his ships to … .
1 ☐ Herculaneum   3 ☐ Stabiae
2 ☐ Rome

g Felix goes on a ship, but … has to stay in Misenum.
1 ☐ Gaius Plinius   3 ☐ Pliny
2 ☐ Alcander

h Gaius Plinius sends his nephew to Rome to tell the … about Vesuvius.
1 ☐ Admiral   3 ☐ Emperor
2 ☐ gods

i The ships can't … Herculaneum because of the wild sea.
1 ☐ reach   3 ☐ see
2 ☐ leave

j They sail further south and Felix thinks that Agathe is … .
1 ☐ free   3 ☐ safe
2 ☐ dead

WORD WORK

Label the pictures with the words from Chapter 8.

balcony   emperor   guard   oar
row   seal   sharp   snake   sword

a .....sharp.....

b ....

c ....

d ....

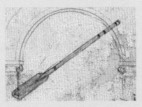

e ....

f ....

g ....

h ....

i ....

GUESS WHAT

What happens in the next chapter? Match the two halves of each sentence.

a Gaius Plinius

b A sailor in Stabiae

c Agathe

d Petrus and Bassus

e Festus, Rectina and Agathe

f Festus

1 stay in Herculaneum.

2 get into a small boat.

3 hits Rectina and she falls into the sea.

4 goes south in the boat alone.

5 dies on the beach at Stabiae.

6 sees a small boat in the sea.

Chapter 9 ∽ By boat and ship

Earlier that afternoon, Festus, Rectina, Agathe, Bassus and Petrus had arrived – after their difficult journey over land – at the port of Herculaneum.

'Get out,' Festus shouted to the others. 'I'm going to find a boat.'

Rectina and Agathe got out of the carriage. Petrus stayed inside with Bassus. There were hundreds of people all along the beach as far as they could see, and a few boats full of people out at sea.

'Let's get back into the carriage, girl,' Rectina said to Agathe. 'At least the stones can't hit us there.'

Rectina got in but Agathe stood with her eyes closed in the middle of the street. Soon Festus came back.

'It's no good. There are no boats left here,' he said to Rectina. 'But what's that crazy young woman doing?'

'Pull her to this side of the street,' said Rectina. 'But don't wake her up. She can see the future. Let's listen,' she added.

Agathe spoke in her strange, low voice.

'I'm lying in a small boat,' she said. 'It's silver and very pretty. The gods are watching me.'

'Just a moment,' said Festus. 'That's it! I forgot the boat we sometimes take out on summer days. The one I keep in the **grotto** in my garden. Only my slaves know about it, and they probably left on foot early this morning when the stones started to fall.'

'Let's use that then,' said Rectina. She opened the carriage door.

'Hurry, Petrus,' she shouted. 'We're going to walk along the beach to Festus's house to get his boat. We'll sail out to sea and meet the navy boats before these other people.'

Petrus climbed out of the carriage with Bassus in his arms. Bassus was trying very hard to stand, but it was clear that he really couldn't walk very far.

grotto a pretty hole in the ground made by people

'Try harder, Father,' said Petrus.

'I'm sorry, son. Something's wrong with my legs. I can't feel them.'

'A life of drinking and running after women has made him weak!' said Rectina. 'Well, we can't carry him – and we must find Festus's boat fast. So let's leave him!'

'No. You go,' answered Petrus. 'I'm staying here – with him.'

'I'll stay with you,' said Agathe, who had opened her eyes again, and was speaking in her usual voice once more.

'Come on, Rectina! Who cares about them?' cried Festus.

Together Festus and Rectina started hurrying along the beach. They had covered their heads with cushions from the carriage to save themselves from the falling stones.

'Go with them,' said Petrus to Agathe.

Agathe looked at him, but did not move.

'Agathe,' said Petrus, 'Admiral Gaius Plinius is coming here with his ships to save us. Don't worry. We'll be fine! But if – by any chance – anything bad happens to me, please ask Felix to tell Flavia how much I loved her. He'll understand the message. Now go and find your boat and Felix.'

With **tears** in her eyes, Agathe kissed Petrus and left him on the beach with his father. She followed Rectina and Festus, but it was difficult with her bad foot. She looked back once. There were people everywhere, running around and shouting, but two men were sitting together calmly in the middle of the crowds. They seemed to

tear the water that comes from your eye when you cry

be happy. It was a picture she always remembered.

By the time she reached Rectina and Festus, Agathe's foot was hurting badly.

'So you've decided to join us!' said Rectina. 'Well, hurry up!'

In half an hour, they reached Festus's garden and found the boat in the grotto. There was nobody at the house, but they sent Agathe for food and water to take with them. She was exhausted when she came back.

Rectina and Festus carried the boat to the beach. Rectina and Agathe got in. Then Festus pushed the boat into the sea, but the waves kept pushing it back. Other people on the beach saw this and started running towards them.

'Get us away from these people!' Rectina shouted at Festus.

Agathe took another oar and tried to help Festus. The boat moved slowly away from the beach.

'Row faster, you idiots!' screamed Rectina.

'Shut up!' shouted Festus against the noise of the wind and the crashing waves.

'Don't talk to me like that!' Rectina screamed back.

Festus hit her angrily with the oar to make her quiet. At the same time, a huge wave hit the boat and Rectina fell into the sea. Agathe saw Rectina's head go under the water. She tried to grab her mistress, but the next wave washed Rectina far away.

'Leave her,' shouted Festus. 'She can swim back to the beach. We must row on.'

The air was getting hotter, and more stones and ash were coming out of the mountain. People on the beach started to walk into the water just because it was cooler. The boat **drifted** south with the wind, but there were people all around them in the sea because they were still near the land. Suddenly one man tried to get into the boat by grabbing Festus's oar. Festus pulled back on the oar, but the man was stronger and he pulled Festus into the sea with him. Agathe was now alone in the boat, which was still moving south. She saw desperate faces all around her in the water, but she was too tired to do anything. She lay down in the bottom of the boat.

'Only the gods can help me now,' she thought, and she closed her eyes and fell asleep.

When Gaius Plinius's ships arrived at Stabiae, more gas and fire came out of Vesuvius.

'I'm going to a friend's house to sleep,' the old admiral told Felix. 'Tomorrow morning we'll save the people of Stabiae. Everyone on the ships needs a rest – you more than anyone, my boy.'

'Thank you, sir,' answered Felix.

He stood and watched Plinius go. How could he sleep? He knew Agathe and Petrus must be dead, and he wanted to die too. Then one of the sailors came out on deck.

'Come inside with me,' he said kindly. 'The hot stones are falling on you out here.'

Felix was too tired to feel anything. He let the sailor take him inside and put him on a bed where he soon fell asleep.

Early the next morning, Gaius Plinius returned to the ships. He was **coughing** badly in the hot, smelly air. Crowds of people were

drift to move here and there on water without using any oars

cough to make a noise in your throat

waiting on the beach to leave. The sailors had told them to wait for the admiral. Plinius looked at the sea. It was still dark and the waves were wilder than before. The terrible smell from the volcano was all around them and it was difficult to breathe. The old man stared at all the people on the beach. He started to walk towards them to explain that they had to sail as soon as they could. Suddenly he fell to the ground. His sailors hurried to help him.

'I can't breathe,' he whispered. 'It's over for me. I'm dying. But you must sail as soon as you can and save all these people. Don't forget your **duty** as sailors in the Emperor's navy.'

The old admiral turned his head towards Vesuvius.

'All of this will stop some time, when the gods decide. Don't give up hope, men.'

He coughed one more time, and then he died there on the hot ash just beside his ships.

Four hours later, Felix woke up. The pillar of ash was still **rising** into the air and it was still strangely dark for the time of day. Felix looked around him. Many people had escaped from the beach at

duty what you must do to be a good person

rise (*past* **rose**, **risen**) to go up

Stabiae. He could see them on the admiral's ship where he was, and on the other Roman ships arranged in a circle in the sea around it. Gaius Plinius's ships were all riding the waves safely a short way from the coast. When Felix looked towards the land where Pompeii had once been, he could see only a desert of black stones through the greyish air. On the beach were many dead bodies. A few people were still alive there. They sat and waited for death to come to them. Felix saw a man and woman **hugging** two children. Fine pieces of ash rained down on them, covering them in a soft thick blanket like hot grey snow.

'Why am I living?' he thought. 'Everyone I love is dead. I should be dead, too.' He thought of Agathe and tears ran down his face.

'What's the matter?' said one of the sailors, looking at him. 'We're lucky. We're still alive. Even Gaius Plinius is dead.'

Suddenly, another sailor shouted, 'A boat!'

A small, silver, rowing boat was drifting slowly towards the ships. It was difficult to see clearly in the half-light coming from the ashy sky, but it seemed to be empty.

hug to take lovingly in your arms

READING CHECK

Tick the correct answers.

a Why do Petrus and Bassus stay on the beach at Herculaneum?

1 ☐ Because Petrus can't swim.

2 ☑ Because Bassus can't walk.

3 ☐ Because Rectina tells them to wait there.

b Why does Agathe go with Festus and Rectina?

1 ☐ Because Petrus tells her to.

2 ☐ Because Rectina orders her to.

3 ☐ Because Bassus asks her to.

c Where does Festus find the small boat?

1 ☐ In the garden of his house.

2 ☐ On the beach.

3 ☐ In the port.

d What happens to Festus and Rectina?

1 ☐ They want to swim to Stabiae.

2 ☐ Agathe pushes them out of the boat.

3 ☐ They fall out into the sea.

e What happens to Gaius Plinius on the beach at Stabiae?

1 ☐ He sails his ships away.

2 ☐ He sleeps inside one of his ships.

3 ☐ He dies on the beach because he can't breathe.

f What has happened to Pompeii when Felix wakes up on the ship?

1 ☐ It has disappeared under stones and ash.

2 ☐ It has disappeared into the sea.

3 ☐ All the people there have escaped to the beaches.

g What does a sailor see coming towards the ships?

1 ☐ A huge wave.

2 ☐ A cloud of smoke and ash.

3 ☐ A small silver boat.

Pompeii today. It was buried under metres of ash and rocks in AD 79.

WORD WORK

Complete the sentences with the correct form of the words above the volcano.

cough

hug

drift

rise

duty

~~grotto~~

tear

a We looked round the pretty little ....g̲r̲o̲t̲t̲o̲.... in the garden.

b I'm too ill to go out. I've got a cold and a bad ....

c There was no wind, so our boat .... into the port.

d The two brothers .... when they met after twenty years.

e .... fell from her eyes as she watched the film's sad ending.

f What time does the sun .... in the morning?

g It's a soldier's .... to fight for his or her country.

GUESS WHAT

What happens in Chapter 10? Match the phrases to make sentences.

a The sailors	**1** becomes	**i** Spurius's business partner.
b Felix and Agathe	**2** like	**ii** and have children.
c Alcander	**3** find Agathe	**iii** in the rowing boat.
d Felix	**4** get married	**iv** in Rome.
e Flavia and Alcander	**5** is at Spurius's house	**v** each other.

CHAPTER 10 ∾ BACK TO ROME

Some sailors went to check the little silver boat. Felix watched without much interest as two sailors got into it.

'There's a young woman here,' one of them shouted. They lifted a **slim** body into their bigger boat. Felix saw that she had long, **blonde** hair. Could it be Agathe? When the sailors carried the blonde-haired figure onto the ship, Felix ran over.

'Agathe!' he shouted. She was with him again! But her eyes were closed and she was very **pale**.

'Is she dead?' he asked.

'Not **quite**,' said a sailor. 'But she needs the ship's doctor.'

Felix followed them while they took Agathe inside.

'Drink,' the doctor said, putting water to her lips.

Agathe **swallowed** and her eyes opened. She saw Felix and smiled. She tried to speak, but no sound came.

'Don't talk,' said the doctor. 'Sleep. Your friend is with you.'

Felix nodded. Agathe looked at him, and he took her hand. Slowly, she closed her eyes again.

'When she wakes up, give her more water,' said the doctor.

While Felix waited by Agathe's side, he realized the ship was moving. The sailors had decided to sail away from Vesuvius with the people they had managed to save. They remembered what their admiral had said. The people needed to be somewhere safe. Also someone must send word to the Emperor.

slim nicely thin

blonde yellow-coloured

pale without a lot of colour

quite fully

swallow to take something from your mouth down into your throat

That evening, when Agathe woke up, she could talk again. She told Felix and the sailors everything she had seen in Pompeii and Herculaneum. The men shook their heads. Felix realized that probably thousands of people had died with Petrus and Bassus.

The ships stopped at the next port along the coast. Messages were sent to Rome. But Agathe and Felix could think only about Alcander at Misenum. They wanted to go to him. But nobody wanted to go anywhere near Vesuvius.

'I think it's best to go to Rome,' answered Felix. 'We must tell Flavia about Petrus. And perhaps Spurius will help us to find Alcander. He's not a bad man. And in Rome I have a job, so we can live there as man and wife... if you still want to marry me.'

Agathe smiled. 'Not even a volcano can change that!'

So Felix and Agathe left the **nightmare** of Pompeii behind.

Two days later, they arrived at Spurius's house. When Felix walked into the hall, he saw Agathe's brother in Spurius's office.

'Where can my sister and Felix be?' he was asking.

'Anywhere,' Spurius answered, 'if they're still alive.'

Felix spoke quietly. He did not want Alcander to be too **shocked.**

'Alcander, we're here.'

The young Greek looked up suddenly.

'Felix – thank the gods – and Agathe?'

'She's outside,' answered Felix.

Alcander hurried out to hug his sister. Felix stood before Spurius. The anger between them was long gone.

'Felix,' said his old master. 'I'm pleased to see you. Cassia will be, too. We're both sorry about that business with the graffiti. Flavia explained it all to us in the end.'

To Felix, that whole story seemed a hundred years ago. 'It's not important,' he said. 'But how did Alcander find you?'

nightmare a bad dream

shocked to feel surprised about something bad

'He remembered my name. He thought you might bring his sister here. He was with Pliny's family. They knew how to find me.'

'How did they leave Misenum?' Felix asked.

'They walked,' said a voice behind Felix. 'Pliny's going to write all about it.'

It was Cassia.

'But how did *you* escape?' she added.

'Cassia,' said Spurius, 'I think Felix should eat and drink before you start questioning him.'

Cassia blushed.

'I'm sorry, Felix,' she said. 'I'll order food and wine at once.'

When Flavia came home from the market, Agathe took her quietly into the garden to tell her about Petrus.

Flavia went to her room for several days after that and saw no one. Then slowly, over the weeks and months that followed, she and Agathe became good friends.

The next spring, Felix married Agathe. He stayed as a partner in the business with Spurius, and Alcander learned how to design and make mosaics, too.

Three years later, Felix and Agathe had two young children, and Felix's mosaics were famous all over Rome. Spurius decided to **retire,** and sold his half of the business to Felix. After that, Flavia often visited the **workshop** to meet Agathe and help with the children. Agathe noticed she liked talking to Alcander, too.

One day, Flavia came into the workshop while Felix was out visiting a customer. She seemed very excited.

'The Emperor wants a mosaic to remember the people of Pompeii and Herculaneum,' she said. 'Everyone thinks he'll ask Felix to design it. It'll be inside an important building in Rome. What do you think, Alcander? Will he do it?'

'I'm not sure,' answered Alcander. 'We don't like to remember

retire to stop working when you are old

workshop a room where you do work with your hands

Pompeii. I still have nightmares about it, you know, even today.'

'I think,' said Agathe slowly, 'that Felix *will* do it – to honour all the people like Petrus who died.'

A dark shadow crossed Flavia's face.

'I hadn't thought of that,' she said.

Flavia sat down, sad and alone. Agathe looked at Alcander. He was watching Flavia worriedly.

'I'll fetch some more wine,' Agathe said, leaving the room. When Felix came home, she stopped him at the workshop door.

'Let's go for a walk with the children,' she said. 'Alcander and Flavia need some time together. And I have exciting news.'

'Why do they need time together?' asked Felix.

'Believe me. They do. Just come with me,' she said. 'It's something a woman understands – and a man never will!'

READING CHECK

Correct ten more mistakes in the chapter summary.

Some of Gaius Plinius's sailors find Agathe in the silver ~~sea~~ *boat*. She sleeps for some time and then wakes and speaks about the things she saw in Stabiae and Herculaneum. The ship stops in the next port and Felix and Agathe get off and travel to Misenum. They go to Pliny's house and find Alcander there. Spurius and Cassia are both angry to see Felix. Felix tells Flavia about Petrus and slowly they become good friends. Felix and Agathe get married and Felix becomes a slave in Spurius's business, and then buys the whole house. Alcander stays in Rome and works with Felix making statues. Flavia likes him and they start to fall in love. Three years later, the Emperor wants to order a drawing to remember the people of Pompeii and Herculaneum. Flavia and Agathe think that Spurius will design and make it.

WORD WORK

Circle the correct words to complete the sentences.

a My sister often has bad (nightmares)/ neighbours at night.

b You look very pain / pale . Do you feel OK?

c He's repairing a car in his workshop / worried at the moment.

d My grandfather returned /retired from work when he was sixty-five.

e She's very slim / skin . I don't think that she eats much.

f Try not to shallow / swallow any water while you are swimming.

g I was shocked / shot by the price. It was very expensive.

WHAT NEXT?

What do you know about Vesuvius and Pompeii? Are the sentences on page 71 true or false? Circle the correct answers.

a More than 2,500,000 million people visit Pompeii every year.

True / False

b We know about what happened in Pompeii from two famous letters written by Pliny.

True / False

c Mount Vesuvius is one of the most dangerous volcanoes in the world.

True / False

d Pompeii was forgotten for **600 years** before it was discovered again by accident.

True / False

e Pompeii is about 80 kilometres away from Mount Vesuvius.

True / False

f Things under the ash stayed as they were in **79 AD**, and we have learnt much about **Ancient Roman** history from them.

True / False

71

Project A *Writing a Diary*

1 **Read the diary entries by the story characters. Answer the questions about each.**

- **Who wrote it?**
- **What story events does it describe?**
- **When and where in the story did he or she write it?**

ⓐ

We arrived here in Pompeii only this morning, but already it feels like we've been here for days. From the port we took a carriage to the baths with the two masters. I felt like a slave again, giving them their towels and doing as they said. Then, Bassus sent Felix and me to open an account at a tile shop in the city centre. I recognized some of the streets, but some places looked completely new. But I found the way there and then to Bassus's house easily enough. His wife met us at the door. She seems a hard woman. Now Felix and I are here in our room.

ⓑ

I'm sitting on the balcony watching my uncle and his ships sail away from Misenum towards Herculaneum. Uncle's a very brave man, and I understand that he feels he must try and save as many people as possible, but his task is very dangerous. Two hours ago, a dirty young man and a slave arrived here to see Uncle. They'd travelled on horse and foot from Pompeii and brought news from people in the city. Now uncle's taking the young man with him and the slave will travel with me to Rome. He seems a good man and he'll help me, I'm sure.

PROJECTS

2 Use these notes to write a diary entry by Felix.

- an extraordinary day
- 1st - finished Caius Lepidus's
  mosaic
- he loved it
- suddenly there was an
  earthquake
- pushed the master away from a
  falling statue
- saved his life - and now I'm a
  freed man!
- collected Petrus on the way home
- fixed two mistakes in his mosaic
- he wasn't happy
- Cassia angry with Spurius when
  we came back home

3 Write another diary entry. Choose a character and a moment in the story.

_____
_____
_____
_____
_____
_____
_____
_____
_____

Project B *A Presentation*

1 Look at the presentation on Ancient Rome. Match the speech bubbles with the slides.

❶

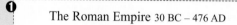

The Roman Empire 30 BC – 476 AD

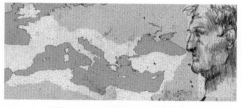

Titus was the Emperor in 79 AD.

ⓐ This is a Roman temple. You can still see it in Rome. It was built for the ancient Roman gods, and it has one of the first domes on it. It took eight years to build.

❷

Homes and Families

Roman family = husband, wife, children, and slaves.
Rich families lived in villas = big houses.

ⓑ For rich Romans, the family was like a small business with slaves as well as children. Roman men had a lot more power than women both in and out of the home.

❸

Architecture

The Pantheon, Rome, 118 – 126 AD
Romans built the first dome.

ⓒ Roman history is divided into three main time periods: before the rise of Rome, the Roman Republic, and the Roman Empire. The Empire period is usually divided up by who was the Emperor.

d

The Romans invented many things to make the lives of rich people more comfortable. They didn't invent many machines, because they had slaves to do all their work!

❹ Leisure

They watched:
– chariot races
– gladiator fights
– theatre, circus, shows
They enjoyed:
– the baths
– ball games, dice
– parties

e

Ancient Romans went to the baths to relax as well as wash. They were a good place to exercise, meet friends and do business. Romans liked horse and chariot races, and gladiator shows, too!

❺ Food

The Romans loved eating!

They ate or drank:	They didn't eat:
– cereals and bread	– potatoes
– olive oil	– tomatoes
– wine	– sugar
– goat's milk, cheese, yoghurt	
– fruit and vegetables	
– snails	
– ice cream	

❻ Technology

Roman aqueducts carried water into cities.

Roman inventions:
arches
concrete
central heating

f

Rich Romans ate wonderful food cooked by slaves. Many poor Romans didn't have kitchens, so they took their food to the baker to cook. There were many take-away food shops in Ancient Rome.

Aztec Chinese Greek Egyptian Inca

2 Choose an ancient civilization. Make notes to plan a slide presentation.

Overview: civilization, places and dates

Leisure

Homes and families

Food

Architecture

Technology

3 Research and prepare the presentation.

GRAMMAR CHECK

Past Simple Active and Passive

When we talk about a past action or event, we usually use the Past Simple Active.

Felix saved Spurius's life.

When we want to focus on a past action and either we do not know who did it, or the person doing the action is not important to us, we can use the Past Simple Passive.

One of the green tiles was broken.

We make the Past Simple Passive with *was/were* + the past participle.

We add information about who or what did the action in a Passive sentence using *by*.

Felix was freed by Spurius.

1 Complete this text using the Past Simple Passive or the Past Simple Active.

Caius Calvinus Lepidus **a)** ...*was pleased*... (please) by what he saw. The mosaic,
which **b)** .... (design) by the slave Felix, **c)** .... (look) beautiful!
Lepidus politely **d)** .... (offer) Spurius some wine, but his offer
e) .... (refuse) just as politely. Then suddenly the whole room
f) .... (shake) by a small earthquake. A large statue **g)** ....
(knock) to the floor by the tremor. Luckily nobody **h)** .... (hurt) because
Felix **i)** .... (push) his master out of the way just in time. After that, Felix
j) .... (give) his freedom by Spurius who **k)** .... (feel) very
grateful to him.
Before they **l)** .... (leave) the senator's house, Spurius and Felix
m) .... (tell) by Lepidus that there had been more than the usual number of
earthquakes south of Rome recently. Then they **n)** .... (go) to collect Petrus
from a house nearby.
When all three of them **o)** .... (arrive) back at Spurius's house in Rome, they
p) .... (met) in the hall by Spurius's wife, Cassia.

GRAMMAR

GRAMMAR CHECK

Relative clauses with *who, what, where, when*

We use *who* to introduce relative clauses about people.

Petrus was the one who had the idea of writing graffiti.

We use *what* to introduce relative clauses about things.

The graffiti was what made Cassia so angry.

We use *where* to introduce relative clauses about places.

The outside wall of Spurius's house was where Petrus wrote the graffiti.

We use *when* to introduce relative clauses about times.

Just after lunch was when Petrus wrote it.

2 Complete these sentences with *who, what, where,* or *when*.

a Asking Spurius if they could marry was ..... what ..... Flavia and Petrus planned to do.

b Spurius's office was .... Cassia spoke to Flavia.

c 'You must marry Felix,' was .... Cassia told her daughter.

d Flavia's screams were .... Petrus heard in the garden.

e Petrus was the one .... loved Flavia.

f The garden was .... Petrus took Flavia in his arms.

g Felix was the person .... said hello to them there

h What the neighbours thought – and said – about her was .... worried Cassia more than anything.

i A bottle of wine was .... Festus and Bassus had in their carriage.

j Festus was the visitor .... had problems walking up the steps.

k Spurius was the only one of the family .... tried to make polite conversation over lunch.

l After lunch was .... Festus and Bassus went to the Colosseum.

m Two hours later was .... Cassia saw the graffiti.

n The fact that the graffiti said she was forty was .... made Cassia really very angry.

GRAMMAR

GRAMMAR CHECK

Used to

We use used to when we talk about past habits. We make the affirmative with used + to + infinitive.

Bassus used to drive a chariot in the races, but he doesn't any more.

We make the negative with didn't + use + to + infinitive.

Bassus didn't use to drink much, but he drinks a lot now.

We make the question with did + subject + use + to + infinitive.

Did Bassus use to play dice when he was younger?

3 Complete these sentences with the *used to* form of the verbs in brackets in the affirmative or negative.

a Bassus ..used to live.. (live) with his parents when he was a young man.

b He .... (be) handsome and very good at sport when he was younger.

c He .... (go) to parties every night because he was so famous.

d He .... (stay) alone at home every evening.

e He .... (have) a very exciting life as a charioteer.

f He .... (feel) that life was boring in those days.

g He .... (have) much money before he married Rectina.

h Rectina .... (watch) the chariot races a lot when Bassus was in them.

i She .... (hate) her husband when they were first married.

j She .... (love) Bassus until she learnt he spent time with other women.

4 Write questions with *used to* using these prompt words.

a Festus and Bassus/be/friends/when/they/be/younger

.Did Festus and Bassus used to be friends when they were younger?.

b Rectina/live/with her parents/before/she/marry/Bassus

....

c Bassus's parents/watch/the chariot races/when/he/be/in them

....

d Petrus's mother/spend/a lot of time with Bassus/before/Petrus/be born

....

e Bassus/see/much of his son/before/he/send/him/away to Rome.

....

GRAMMAR

GRAMMAR CHECK

Past Continuous and Past Simple

We often use the Past Continous to describe things or talk about repeated past actions.

Petrus and Felix were standing on one side of the square. (= **describing**)

Felix was looking around him interestedly. (= **talking about repeated actions**)

We use the Past Simple to describe single actions in the past, and for state verbs (like have, seem, want) which we can't use in the continuous form.

Petrus put a hand on Felix's arm. (= **single action**)

Petrus had Bassus's letter to the shop owner with him. (= **state verb**)

5 **Complete the text with the verbs in the box in the Past Continuous where possible, or in the Past Simple.**

buy	carry	give	have	leave	look	pay	see
sell	not seem	stand	~~speak~~	stop	talk	wear	want

The people around them **a)** ..*were speaking*.. different languages, and some of them **b)** .... to be Roman. The shops **c)** .... fruit and vegetables that Felix hadn't seen before.

Just then, across the square, Felix **d)** .... a beautiful slave girl. She **e)** .... a blue tunic, and she **f)** .... yellow hair and blue eyes. She **g)** .... a basket over one arm, and she **h)** .... some fruit from one of the shops in the market. She and the shop owner **i)** .... together in a friendly way while she **j)** .... him for the fruit.

Suddenly the girl **k)** .... across the square at Felix. She **l)** .... him a smile, and then she **m)** .... the square in a hurry with her basket of fruit. Felix **n)** .... to run after her at once, but Petrus, who **o)** .... next to him, **p)** .... him from following her.

80

GRAMMAR CHECK

Direct and reported speech

In direct speech we give the words that people say.	In reported speech we put the verb a step into the past and we change the pronouns and time and place references.

'Neptune is angry,' said Agathe.   *Agathe said (that) Neptune was angry.*

'The gods will punish us!' she said.   *She said (that) the gods would punish them.*

We can use the word that to introduce reported speech statements, but it is not necessary.

tell needs an indirect object – me, her, Felix; say does not need an indirect object.

Alcander told Felix (that) it was the most beautiful mosaic he had ever seen.

He said (that) it was the most beautiful mosaic he had ever seen.

We use tell + infinitive with *to* to report commands, and ask + infinitive with *to* to report requests.

'Pull back the curtain,' Bassus said to Felix.   *Bassus told Felix to pull back the curtain.*

'Please look at it,' he said to his guests.   *He asked his guests to look at it.*

6 **Rewrite the direct speech sentences in reported speech.**

a 'Please play dice with me for Agathe's freedom,' Felix said to Bassus.

Felix asked Bassus to play dice with him for Agathe's freedom

b 'If I lose the game, I'll be your slave,' Felix explained to Bassus.

....

c 'You can't refuse to play in front of all your guests,' Rectina told Bassus.

....

d 'Bring me the dice,' Bassus told Alcander.

....

e 'He's a brave boy,' said the senator's wife of Felix.

....

f 'You have some friends in high places,' the general told Felix.

....

g 'I've won your freedom,' Felix told Agathe.

....

h 'Please choose a couch for dinner,' said Rectina to everybody.

....

GRAMMAR CHECK

Gerund with sense verbs

We use the -ing verb form (the gerund) with verbs of the senses like hear, see, feel and smell, and also verbs like watch, listen to and notice.

Suddenly they heard lots of dogs howling.

When a verb ends in consonant + e, we remove the final e and add -ing

come – coming, shake – shaking

When a verb ends in consonant + short vowel + single consonant, we double the final consonant and add -ing

hit – hitting, run - running

With the verbs die and lie we remove the final ie and add -ying

die – dying, lie - lying

7 Complete the sentences with the verbs in brackets in the *–ing* form

a They saw smoke ...*coming*... (come) from Vesuvius.

b They felt the ground .... (shake) under them.

c The horses felt stones .... (hit) their backs.

d Petrus felt his father .... (lie) across him.

e Agathe noticed people .... (run) around.

f She heard people .... (scream), ... (shout), and .... (cry).

g She saw Petrus and Bassus .... (sit) calmly in the middle of the crowd.

h Agathe and Festus noticed people .... (swim) in the sea around their boat.

i Felix and Alcander saw some people .... (hide) in their houses.

j They heard officers in Misenum .... (give) orders to slaves.

k Felix heard people .... (die) in Herculaneum.

l He smelt the gas .... (come) from the volcano in Stabiae.

m The sailors heard Gaius Plinius .... (whisper) as he lay on the beach.

n Felix saw the ships around him .... (ride) the waves near the coast.

o He noticed a man and a woman .... (hug) two children under a blanket of ash on the beach.

p He watched two sailors .... (get) into the little silver boat.